21 Poems

NEW DIRECTIONS POETRY PAMPHLETS

George Oppen

21 Poems

Edited by David B. Hobbs

NEW DIRECTIONS POETRY PAMPHLET #21

Cover design by Erik Carter
Interior design by Eileen Baumgartner and Erik Rieselbach
Manufactured in the United States of America
New Directions Books are printed on acid-free paper
First published as New Directions Poetry Pamphlet #21 in 2017

Library of Congress Cataloging-in-Publication Data
Names: Oppen, George. | Hobbs, David B., editor.
Title: 21 poems / edited by David Hobbs.
Other titles: Twenty one poems
Description: New York, NY : New Directions Publishing, 2017. |
Series: New Directions poetry pamphlet
Identifiers: LCCN 2017009771 | ISBN 9780811226912 (acid-free paper)
Classification: LCC PS3529.P54 A6 2017 | DDC 811/.52—dc23
LC record available at https://lccn.loc.gov/2017009771

10 9 8 7 6 5 4 3 2

ndbooks.com

New Directions Books are published for James Laughlin
by New Directions Publishing Corporation
80 Eighth Avenue, New York 10011

The Oppens on their boat in California, c. 1930

The envelope containing 21 Poems *sent to Pound from Zukofsky*

Introduction

On March 6, 1930, Louis Zukofsky wrote to Ezra Pound:

> I may have 32pp of poems by George Oppen for you—He seems
> to me to handle a kind of void in a way all his own—so that
> one excuses the posited negatives, the occasional Cummings
> and confused perceptions.

Six weeks later, Zukofsky sent an assemblage by the then-twenty-
one-year-old poet, which reached Pound in Paris. It was an unbound
sheaf of typewritten poems varying dramatically in voice and style,
one per page, with the heading "21 Poems by George Oppen" hand-
written in pencil on the first page.

At the time, Oppen was a young husband and college dropout,
recently returned to California from New York City. Though born
in New Rochelle, New York, Oppen spent most of his youth in the
San Francisco area, where his father owned several movie theaters.
During his brief time at Oregon Agricultural College (now Oregon
State University), he and Mary Oppen (née Colby) were introduced
by their English professor, Jack Lyons—the same professor who
George credited with introducing him to "such a thing as modern
poetry other than what I had been writing." George and Mary
eloped in Dallas on October 7, 1927—George under the assumed
name "David Verdi." By the winter of 1928, the Oppens were living
in Manhattan and were introduced to Zukofsky shortly after find-
ing his "Poem beginning 'The'" in Pound's magazine, *The Exile*, at
the Gotham Book Mart.

On April 8, 1929, Oppen gained access to a small inheritance
from his mother's estate for his twenty-first birthday. He and Mary
planned to move to France and start a small press. There, they

would use the same printer in Dijon who had produced James Joyce's *Ulysses* for Sylvia Beach of Shakespeare and Company, and with Zukofsky formed To Publishers—"when questioned we say something about the dative," George wrote to Pound—bringing out collections of prose by William Carlos Williams and Pound, as well as *An "Objectivists" Anthology*, which included their own poems as well as work by Basil Bunting, Mary Butts, Frances Fletcher, T. S. Eliot, Carl Rakosi, Kenneth Rexroth, Charles Reznikoff, and others. But before leaving for Europe, the Oppens first moved back to California: "We wanted to spend a year in San Francisco writing and assimilating our New York experience," Mary wrote in her autobiography, *Meaning a Life* (1978). It was during this stay, while he and Mary lived in a bohemian waterfront community in Sausalito, across Richardson Bay from his father in Belvedere, that Oppen sent *21 Poems* to Zukofsky.

Zukofsky wrote another letter to Pound on June eighteenth of that year:

> No noos from you re-Geo. Oppen's poems. Shd.
> have mentioned his contribution of 'everything
> brightly not there' in all his poems, in the
> essay enclosed—but then he's not been published.

Pound did not seem to have had any "noos" to share, and whether it was due to difficulty, busyness, or indifference, he would not mention Oppen to Zukofsky until arrangements for publishing his prose collection *How to Read* (1932) were underway. We might even detect an apology in Zukofsky mentioning "he's not been published"— just four of the original poems Pound received would see print during Oppen's lifetime. But Pound kept the typescript, and it remained with the Ezra Pound Foundation until 1990, when it was acquired by Yale University's Beinecke Library as a part of the sale of Olga Rudge's papers, and archived in one of the many Pound collections that they have preserved.

In the summer of 2015, I went to the Beinecke with a difficult question. I had been researching the relationship between city life and conceptions of "the lyric" and was working on a chapter about George Oppen's *Discrete Series* (1934), a book that remains enigmatic even eighty years after its initial publication. A group of thirty-one short, mostly untitled poems that evoke the experience of modernity but prefer subtlety and syntactic contortion to direct emotional expression, *Discrete Series* received astonishing support upon release. Pound contributed a preface that concluded: "I salute a serious craftsman, a sensibility which is not every man's sensibility and which has not been got out of any other man's books." William Carlos Williams wrote a glowing review of it for *Poetry* magazine, praising Oppen as "a 'stinking' intellectual" whose verse rests "on a craftsmanlike economy of means," and went on to predict that Oppen's work would push readers to remember that "poems are constructions." But their shared awe of Oppen's craftsmanship was not broadly predictive. The poems themselves appear rather seamless and gnomic, leaving readers with few clues as to how to read them. For the most part, the poem sequence has been seen as a kind of momentary eruption rather than a slow accumulation of effort—a brief poetic apprenticeship before Oppen turned to political activism and chose not to write any poetry for almost twenty-five years.

The resulting tendency has been to imagine Oppen's first book as a singular composition, emphasizing "series" at the expense of "discreteness." Here, Oppen himself would eventually offer a corrective. Writing to Rachel Blau DuPlessis in 1965, he commented:

Discrete Series—a series in which each term is empirically justified rather than derived from the preceding term. Which is what the expression means to a mathematician, as I gather you know.

(I thought too late—30 years too late—that the flyleaf should have carried the inscription 14, 28, 32, 42 which is a discrete series: the names of the stations on the east side subway.

Riding the train end-to-end may tell us about the geographic distance between stations, even about the extent of the city, but it reveals little about those places where we may disembark. Likewise, each poem in *Discrete Series* is built around its own logic, though the lack of supporting indication of where that logic comes from or how it is operating means that we often rely on the next poem to interpret it. Oppen was fond of quoting the following lines by Reznikoff: "Coming up the subway stairs, I thought the moon / only another street-light— / a little crooked."

As Oppen's political convictions whisked him around the United States, then to France and Germany in the Second World War (where he was wounded), back to New York, and then to California, he came to the attention of the FBI. The first entry in his heavily-redacted file is dated 1941: "The subject was Kings County election campaign manager for Communist Party in 1936 elections. Voted Communist Party ticket in 1936....Subject not found and therefore not being considered for custodial detention." Oppen couldn't be found because he was already in Detroit, working as a patternmaker in the Machinists Union, and then in Louisiana, where he received basic training. FBI surveillance increased after he returned from the war until a dramatic confrontation with two agents in early 1950, at their home in Redondo Beach, led the Oppens to flee to Mexico. Whatever correspondence or manuscripts George had maintained from the 1930s were lost in the urgency of their departure, and as a result, there has been little in the way of surviving material to provide us with insight into what he was thinking and reading as he wrote *Discrete Series*. I visited the Beinecke with the hope that Zukofsky and Pound, both of whom were in correspondence with Oppen, would have discussed his early writings in their extensive exchange.

What I found was something far more exciting than I could have imagined: an early Oppen manuscript. Scholars have long assumed that the "32pp" to which Zukofsky referred in 1930 comprised a draft of *Discrete Series* that had been lost, like the sheaf he sent to Reznikoff in late 1933, now held in the Archive for New Poetry at the University of California, San Diego. But my recovery of *21 Poems* evinces a larger, more dynamic body of work. Only one poem in the typescript can be found in *Discrete Series*—the final poem, "The mast" — but Oppen published (and tried to publish) these poems for several years after sending them to Pound, suggesting that elements of both collections coexisted for a period of time. In fact, the second, fifth, sixteenth, and twenty-first poems were originally published together as four sections of a different "Discrete Series." We can now understand Zukofsky's scare-quoted "everything brightly not there" to be a reference to the collection's fifteenth poem, while in a broader sense see these poems as precursors to *Discrete Series* in theme and approach. Oppen's love for his young bride, his love of sailing, his skepticism about the impact of modern finance and technology on social life, are evident in both sets. Some of the earlier poems seem like the Imagistic experiments that readers might have expected from an acolyte of Pound, tempered with a Williams-esque fascination with everydayness ("One remembers the smell of warm paint").

But there are also many differences between the two. Although *Discrete Series* includes several poems about seafaring, rural highways, and the metropolis, it rarely seeks to bridge the conceptual distance between these disparate living spaces. (Williams noted "the colors, images, moods [that] are not suburban.") The work in *21 Poems*, however, often seeks a resolution outside of the urban setting. As a whole, this earlier collection has a much greater breadth of tone and mood, and certain poems function in rhetorically theatrical ways that *Discrete Series* rarely allows. Some even read like burlesques of poetic clichés ("The moon rose like a rising moon") or as critiques of cosmopolitan habits ("Your coat slips smoothly from your shoulders to the waiter: / How, in the face of this, shall we remember").

21 Poems also includes more individuals who are identifiable beyond a spare "he" or "she" pronoun, some of whom are addressed with remarkable intimacy ("Here put your head, that desires nothing except familiarly"). These poems eagerly display a skeptical intelligence and turn to irony to comment on the scenes they describe. The first of the earlier sequence, which dramatizes the experience of giving birth, is by far the longest of Oppen's early career. It is nearer a poem like "Parturition" by Mina Loy, who the Oppens would eventually meet in New York, than anything about fatherhood written by other male modernists. The poem shifts constantly between narration, exclamation, and query—the total effect more impressionistic than "objective."

Without a doubt, there is going to be a lot to say about *21 Poems*. There has been a recent surge in Oppen scholarship, supported by published volumes of interviews (*Speaking with George Oppen*, edited by Richard Swigg), prose (*Selected Prose, Daybooks, and Papers*, edited by Stephen Cope), and reminiscences from the Oppens' many friends (*The Oppens Remembered*, edited by DuPlessis). But this is the first publication of new material that precedes Oppen's storied twenty-five years of silence between the publication of *Discrete Series* and his next book, *The Materials*, in 1962. In the back of this pamphlet, I've also included a short "Documents" section of Oppen ephemera that relates to *21 Poems*: a previously-unpublished list Oppen sent to Pound at the end of 1931, in which he describes the literary magazines he was reading; a letter he sent to Williams in early 1932, discussing the printing of Williams's *A Novelette and Other Prose* as well as *21 Poems*; and a letter sent to Pound in February 1934, in which he talks about *Discrete Series* and gives Pound advice for the preface that he would contribute. More importantly, *21 Poems* nearly doubles the size of Oppen's early and influential corpus, and happily, the poems themselves are fascinating. The simple act of sending them to Pound indicates Oppen's ambition, as well as Zukofsky's confidence in his younger friend's work. When I first shared my find with one of my professors, he grabbed my shoulders and said, "Don't get used to this feeling, David, it may never happen again."

—

I am grateful to Linda Oppen for allowing me to bring these poems into print—her trust and enthusiasm have been as important to this project as her formal permission of publication. I appreciate all of the help provided to me by the staff of the Beinecke, especially Nancy Kuhl. The typescript for *21 Poems* is held in the Ezra Pound Papers Addition in the Yale Collection of American Literature at the Beinecke Rare Book and Manuscript Library (YCAL Series 53, Series III, Box 40, Folder 930). All Louis Zukofsky material is copyright Paul Zukofsky; the material may not be reproduced, quoted, or used in any manner whatsoever without the explicit and specific permission of the copyright holder. The Department of English at New York University generously provided the travel funding that allowed me to visit Oppen's archive at the University of California, San Diego, and I received indispensable insight and guidance from professors Phillip B. Harper, Jini Kim Watson, and Rachael Wilson. At New Directions, Jeffrey Yang provided a heroic level of support and Barbara Epler made me feel at home. I must also thank Jaimie MacIsaac for her love and support, without which this work could not have progressed. Finally, I cannot overstate the many debts I owe to Michael Davidson, Rachel Blau DuPlessis, and Peter Nicholls. Thank you.

—DAVID B. HOBBS

I

Round muscles in the damp womb
Move. Child (folded, articulated: knees bent, back rounded)
Fills the dark wholly. Knee jerks shortly, entirely silent.
Surges of blood in the smaller veins beat perhaps now more sharply.
       Begins--
(Hand jumps against the soft wall)--

But for the bound darkness,
Back, back sinking!
The dark pressure, slowly absolute.
Lurches (soundless). Forced muscle to muscle
Pressed blind ungroping, parting the live personal flesh.
That is it! (The woman screaming) Round baby-head to the battered light
      (O God she)
(But dawned in the veins unmoved and unremarkably warm)
New light blunts on the body, shatters in vacant eyes. Shot thru
    already
This stuff with fragile passages. Light has delicate forceps.

The world leaps against the wall,
Spread shapes, colours dissolving. This has been standing
How long, in the waiting light, visible?
      Born! Pulses accurately,
      Surges down soft wrists.

Begins unhesitating.
(Of all we three only) Damp throat beneath, firm with muscles. To
    which
Born? (No return. The woman
Again the woman. The path sealed, no dark pool of comfort.)
The woman returns. Here dropped the world.
But the warm breasts, drawing from inward,
(The round muscles, the ribbed cavern, untaut, unsuspended)
Life irrevocably bright. But the warm breasts, outreached,
Have followed him.

I

Round muscles in the damp womb
Move. Child (folded, articulated: knees bent, back rounded)
Fills the dark wholly. Knee jerks shortly, entirely silent.
Surges of blood in the smaller veins beat perhaps more sharply.
        Begins—
(Hand jumps against the soft wall) —

But for the bound darkness,
Back, back sinking!
The dark pressure, slowly absolute.
Lurches (soundless). Forced muscle to muscle
Pressed blind ungroping, parting the live personal flesh.
That is it! (The woman screaming) Round baby-head to the battered light
        (O God she)
(But dawned in the veins unmoved and unremarkably warm)
New light blunts on the body, shatters in vacant eyes. Shot thru
        already
This stuff with fragile passages. Light has delicate forceps.

The world leaps against the wall,
Spread shapes, colours dissolving. This has been standing
How long, in the waiting light, visible?
        Born! Pulses accurately,
        Surges down soft wrists.

Begins unhesitating.

(Of all we three only) Damp throat beneath, firm with muscles. To
             which
Born? (No return. The woman
Again the woman. The path sealed, no dark pool of comfort.)
The woman returns. Here dropped the world.
But the warm breasts, drawing from inward,
(The round muscles, the ribbed cavern, untaut, unsuspended)
Life irrevocably bright. But the warm breasts, outreached,
Have followed him.

II

This room,
               the circled wind
Straight air of dawn
                       low noon
The darkness. Not within
The mound of these
                 Is anything
To fit the prying of your lips,
Or feed their wide bright flowering.

And yet will movement so exactly fit
Your limbs—
            As snow
Fills the vague intricacies of the day, unlit
Before; so will your arms
                   Fall in the space
Assigned to gesture

           (In the momentless air,
           The distant, adventurous snow)

G.A.Oppen
Sausalito, Cal.

This a ^

~~This~~ A vacant lot;
^Impenetrable ground
Of embedded stones,
Bottle-glass.
My shoes grow
Dusty, not of soil.

No nor ^   ~~Nor yet~~ elsewhere. Simply
and ^   ^This, ~~and~~ my dissatisfaction.

Between eyes and shoes, a plane,
A spaced companiomship, opposing
~~This~~ ~~This dust~~, and some immovable watchfulness.
^

^ *This dust*

III

This a vacant lot;
Impenetrable ground
Of embedded stones,
Bottle-glass.
My shoes grow
Dusty, not of soil.

No nor elsewhere. Simply
This, and my dissatisfaction.

Between eyes and shoes, a plane,
A spaced companionship, opposing
This dust, and some immovable watchfulness.

IV

From here I can easily see
A huge flat red face and iron-grey hair
With mottled buoyancy allowing its two nice hands to place

      Three

   Clear
Packages of

  CAMELS

In a Gladstone

Bag.

V

When, having entered—

Your coat slips smoothly from your shoulders to the waiter:

How, in the face of this, shall we remember;
Should you stand suddenly upon your head

Your skirts would blossom downward

Like an anemone.

VI

The moon rose like a rising moon,
And you beside me sitting silent, or as silently,

Turned, as one who turns, to say,
How beautiful it is; as who should say, How beautiful
It is.

Your lips too red for lips,
Your nose not always like a nose;
I love you as I love
You,
     as I
Love.

VII

If my body were like yours—

I would be alone. With dragging fingers find the hollow
                between breast and shoulder.

Close hips, close legs straightening down the sheets—

Piercing in maidenhair, a candle in my own similar hand

Would fittingly excite me.

VIII

It has been china, then—
Thin and smooth and delicately figured in meticulous line.
And we shall think of teas and a vague trend;
A leaf, caught breathlessly on air:
So shall we think of her,
A fine tracery intricately planned on air,
And walls declining tastefully to hedges.
We shall think of her and teas and china laughter,
Life a trifle thin about the edges.
For the rest, it may be,

Strange, but poised to china dignity,
She shall go down, she shall go down—
A small handful, pitifully,
Of somewhat rose-tinged dust.

G.A.Oppen
Sausalito, Cal.

IX

~~Lobby~~

The revolving door swings load after load into the lobby;
There is a sound of secrets,
A scattering of feet, a crossing, recrossing.
But now, with the sudden weight of prophecy,
Incredibly caught stillness,
The carpet level to the door. From outside,
Short clatter of a street-car- a policeman's whistle
Barely heard.
            Now first visible,
Steadily back and forth,
Past and past the newsboy (straining, silent),
Unvaryingly waiting, overcoated,
Walks the doorman. As in a dark house
A wicker chair craks suddenly in the attic.
            ∧

IX

The revolving door swings load after load into the lobby;
There is a sound of secrets,
A scattering of feet, a crossing, recrossing.
But now, with the sudden weight of prophecy,
Incredibly caught stillness,
The carpet level to the door.   From outside,
Short clatter of a street-car— a policeman's whistle
Barely heard.
                    Now first visible,
Steadily back and forth,
Past and past the newsboy (straining, silent),
Unvaryingly waiting, overcoated,
Walks the doorman.   As in a dark house
A wicker chair cracks suddenly in the attic.

X

Why does this woman talk brightly in an evening-dress,
Whereas some carry huge vanity bags, into which, (and
                    a mirror) they powder
Excitedly?

XI

Drift of shining small fish hangs low over the fine sand
Soft to shadow:
High at the tank's top eel-like fish turn upward, showing clowns
                    soft white faces.
        Three shadowless and accurately finned huge fish mysteriously
                        suspended; untouched, unadventurous,
Drift untwitching above the
Minnows (silent),
And stop, with noses held to

                    Adequate, dissolving points.

XII

Here put your head, that desires nothing except familiarly:
There your feet, bending your knees so that, bare (I remember
    from childhood), they would smell salt-sweet.

There have been women, but of course you are not any one
    of these.
Have you any idea that of a thousand women you are one, and
    of two thousand also one?

And as many men. One's brief and sudden self
Howsoever slowly time passes.

XIII

Gaunt streets bristle toward the cathedral;
      Fear, hate of this tall white weakness.

Four steps lead to the doorway, and the shutter is open at the window,
And solitude dives like a swallow to the high window— the priest
            has said a prayer for those at sea.

   (But not the priest in a prayer of white marble: the tangled
            streets and knotted eyes supplicate, in some grey crowded
            way, the raveled sea)

And solitude, unbroken to the window.

XIV

The light unadvancing thru unregainable unterraced heights,
And the world accepted into the old renewed grey tunnels of the air,
         so that the trees are rootless and too suddenly dead.
The ways, the perishable suppleness.
Such a thing is in my mind as in the square rooms of a city during night.
         Men stumble in the dark
On blindness or on sourceless streams of sight.

So the thin, unstreaming
Glare of the ocean.—

         A private world, insufficiently filled.

Tree of space, unblossoming, O clamp down harder your long skinny stron
         strength
And the earth grow limited beneath me
With an inagility I understand.

XV

One remembers the smell of warm paint:
Bread and butter left on the wood step of the porch.

Round clouds above;
Between,
Everything very brightly
Not there.

XVI

As I lift the glass to drink,
I smell the water:
Suddenly, the summer.

When my socks will be thick in my shoes

And the room's noise will go dim behind me

As I lean out a high window,
My hands on the stone.

XVII

The search-light
Diagonal: (the

Short, but wide night).

XVIII

Now pray the walled world
Heavily to open its low doors
And let walk forth across the pavement
As space swells and drops, some actual uprisen man, woman—
(Not the slight building tops unclasped mid-high in the incoherent
Day, nor globular stars shall margin it).

Bare,
        To receive and quench
The thin paths of venture.

In fields the silence hard between your breasts—.
Your breath is rhythmically whole, filling your wide dark supple
(Pool-like) silent chest.
                          Your hands are caught in webs
And quick. They stitch, I think,
The air and earth together. Stiff-fingered on my lips
They draw a gossamer round belly of air to me,
Between your round light fingers quick to drink.

XIX

The pigeons fly from the dark bough unleaved to the
      window ledge. There is no face
There visible.

XX

So he stood on the island— over the sea
Until creation was a cone with polished sides.

Starring— a man before a bill-board.

Looked to where the shallow-edged sea drew at a pebble, white
Whole; pebble even nowhere. Emerged
Clearly into solitude.
                              He

Possibly saw creation

Barely curve the water,

Circumscribe his unshaping feet.

We, you and I, will go all over the world.
Will feel minutely, adequately heavy as a curving kite-string from a
        hill.
Fields, the porches of houses, the cornered ways of cities—

We will walk everywhere as at each step our toes spread on grass.

    Heads above them, interval planed by chins.

On the island (if he smiled ever smiled)

Sank his feet slightly into sand. Filling nothing.

XXI

The mast
Inaudibly soars; bole-like, tapering:
Sail flattens beneath the wind.
The limp water holds the boat's round sides. Sun
Slants dry light on the deck.

       Beneath us glide
Rocks, sand, and unrimmed holes.

George A. Oppen
le Beausset (Var)
France

Publications in English

Blues

Publishes excellent work: its list of contributors includes Williams, Zukofsky, Rexroth, Gertrude Stein, Nancy Butts, Robert McAlmon. Some other work published seems to indicate that the editors are interested primarily in modern mannerism. Even assuming that to be true, the magazine is undoubtedly useful as removing the necessity for magazines with that purpose. Many would wish, however, that there should be indicated some distinction between the work of Williams and work still relying for distinction chiefly on "modernity".

Pagany

Publishes work by the group of authors also represented in Blues (tho they can be classified as a group only by a similarity in degree of merit), but maintains that standard more consistently.

The New Review

Published in France. Also contains the best of available work; some reproductions of drawings. Is incidentally more successful or less inhibited in explaining itself to the "general public" than are most magazines of its class. A certain mysticism in historical sense (an attempt to date Romantic art, etc.) aiding.

The same company is bringing out an Objectivists' Anthology, edited by Louis Zukofsky.

George Oppen
le Beausset (Var)
France

Hound and Horn

Is ordinarilly described as scholarly. Certainly can be relefd on for an intelligent and informed attitude. Has published prose and verse by Zukofsky, Paul Valery, Ezra Pound, and others.

To, Publishers

A new press, printing in France. Publishes chiefly brochures to sell for 8 Francs. Its program for the year includes: Prolegomena (collected prose) of Ezra Pound (to be published as in a series); A Novelette and Other Prose, by William Carlos Williams; a novel by Charles Reznikoff; poems by Louis Zukofsky. øⁿd/ⁿ/ⁿⁿⁿøⁿⁿⁿⁿøⁿ/øⁿ

American Mercury

H. L. Menken, the editor (whose attitude is closely followed by all work in the magazine), has defended himself against the charge of being "merely destructive". He deals with the stupidity of churoh societies, small town administrations, mid-western senators, and so forth. The ideal left unchallenged is apparently urbanity, or a virile cosmopolitanism. Obviously, Mr. Menken feels that the confession of enjoying "after all" a good glass of beer or a good burleque show as much as anything acquires special force in the mouth of a proffessional intellectual. He is said to have a large following among college students, and is probably in accord with the most intelligent to be found in any number. It would not be accurate to say that the magazine is devoted to advertis-ing, but it is probably felt that the justification of its existence

George Oppen
le Beausset (Var)
France

is indicated by the price it is able to charge for space.

Poetry, A Magazine of Verse

A fairly conservative publication. Nevertheless often of
interest.

Contempo

A magazine concerned with liberal or radical political theses.
A late issue is devoted to the Scotsboro Case-- the trial of six
negroes in Alabama, an obvious case of railroading. The same issue
has a poem by Countee Cullen and work by other negro writers. It lists
as contributors, among others; Sherwood Anderson, Gamaliel Bradford,
John Dos Passos, J. Middleton Murry, Ezra Pound, James Stevens. It
has praised or declared allegiance to William Carlos Williams, Kenneth
Burke, Benjamin de Casseres, and Eugene O'Njel.

Dear Williams:

I enjoyed the "trouble" very much, out of admiration for the book. So don't, as they say, mention it.

I was fairly pleased with the looks of the book myself, aside from one or two obviously regrettable faults (the printer regularly acts contrary to instructions at the last moment, and is careless intermittently). The price, which we were forced to raise constantly before publication, makes a difference of course. If the books were to sell for 2o¢ as we'd originally planned, they would look "neat". "Lushness" was always entirely out of the question; they could, I'm afraid, be better without being de luxe nor obscuring the pressing almost to journalistic nature of the text. That is, without seeming bibliophiles' items.

The round characters I thought were good with the text-- in fact, I like it better yet in typescript (which means also that the type should have been more widely spaced, which we couldn't afford). I'm enclosing the first page of the Ms. in which the thing is most marked so that you can see what I mean.

However, Pound and others seem to feel that the publications should look more proffessional, I think it is, so forthcoming books will be different. If we've experimented at your expense it was absolutely unforseen.

Thanks for the book, which hasn't arrived yet-- your letter arrived just now.

I was very pleased--naturally-- with what you say of my work.
And that "they will not think it aesthetic": is "they" the public
(what the poems do lack, I think, is the dimension of reading-- the
direction in which one reads; that is to say, they do not and are
not really intended to create an environment, so that if reading is
to "fill time"- enuf to matter-- I can see that they are not very
desirable). Or does "they" mean co-editors? in which case you mean
that you can let me know-- or they will let me know if you can use
the work. If you will understand that I appreciate your letter, I
I'd nevertheless like to ask you to _tell_ me more definitely if
you might use the poems. Not necessarily if you will, but if you
might. Which is what you write-- that you might-- but without in
the least feeling that you are over-tactful for what would be pec-
uliarly foolish reasons, I think that because your letter was also
to thank me (for nothing, as I said), you might almost be forced
to a considerable indefiniteness in refusal. And I'd really like
to send the poems elsewhere if you will not be able to use them.

     "If you _might_" because I'd preferthem to be in Contact.
If you simply wish time to decide I certainly don't mind.

               Sincerely
               George Oppen

meanwhile the enclosed - unfinished
when the others were sent!

Feb 9 [1934]

Dear Pound:

I might have answered your letter at more leisure--

‖Yessir, a longer preface would overbalance. Section1 dealing with
wh'll find me shockingly modern will probably never reach those it's
addressed to. But I'm glad to have it along on the chance. Some
little egg might ----. 2 does me heart good (deals with originality-
in-doing-nothing and the tracing of derivations). I think I told you
about the New Yorker who'd been converted to Functionalism. he told me;
whereby he xxx so admired the skyscrapers he wanted to build one on the
Arizona desert for a monument.

        The book'll be named Discrete Series. Tricky, but I want
a name out of statistics for X "Party Aboard" and some others partic-
ularly, and the term describes my hon. intentions pretty acurately.

        "The glass of windows and a family ~~~~~~~~ laundry"--
Yes, I mean laundry on a line. Are there any installed tubs in these
parts? Not too good a poem-- put it in because it emphasizes the
discreteness of the series-- since when I write straight desciption
(there should be a better word for it) it has the same tone as the
more argumentative woiks. And goes into the book just there.

        Not so discrete, they not, -- in the other sense,

                    OPPEN

which, I see 'laundry''s not the
word --

Notes

"21 Poems by George Oppen" penciled in cursive script on the first page of the typescript. Continuous Roman numerals penciled at the top of each page (I–XXI). Edits written in ink appear on nine of the poems. As this typescript passed through the hands of both Zukofsky and Pound, it is possible that any or all of these annotations could have been made by them. It seems more likely, however, that the edits were made by Oppen himself. Many correct misspellings, or eliminate words only to then restore them by hand. The consistency of the notational hand also suggests that all of the edits were made by the same person, and the nature of the changes make it seem more likely that they were though out by a poet finessing his work, rather than by an editor who initially thought a word should be removed, only to then think otherwise. Therefore I have incorporated all handwritten edits, including corrections of spelling, into the poems in this pamphlet. Edits adding or removing whole words—particularly the three struck-out titles —are noted below.

ROUND MUSCLES IN THE DAMP WOMB
See fascimile image of typescript on page 15.

THIS ROOM
"~~Previously~~" is written in ink above the thirteenth line and there is a marking suggesting it would have gone between "day" and "unlit," were it not struck out.

"~~Before~~" appears typed at the beginning of the next line, while a handwritten "Before;" appears in the left-hand margin.

THIS A VACANT LOT
See fascimile image of typescript on page 19.

IT HAS BEEN CHINA, THEN——

Typed title "Prophecy in Pastels" crossed out.

THE REVOLVING DOOR SWINGS LOAD AFTER LOAD INTO THE LOBBY

See fascimile image of typescript on page 26.

GAUNT STREETS BRISTLE TOWARD THE CATHEDRAL

Typed title "Inland" crossed out.

DOCUMENTS (1931–1934)

List of "Publications in English" by George Oppen sent to Ezra Pound (late 1931)—located in the Ezra Pound Papers, YCAL MSS 43, Box 38, Folder 1613, Beinecke Library, Yale University.

Letter from George Oppen to William Carlos Williams (early 1932)—located in the William Carlos Williams Papers, YCAL MSS 116, Box 17, Folder 547, Beinecke Library, Yale University.

Letter from George Oppen to Ezra Pound (February 1934)—located in the Ezra Pound Papers, YCAL MSS 43, Box 38, Folder 1613, Beinecke Library, Yale University.